How to not care what other people think

How to not care what other people think

By

Nancy Sungyun

How to Not Care What People Think

By Nancy Sungyun

Copyright © 2020 by Nancy Sungyun

Published and distributed in the United States.

All rights reserved. Absolutely no part of this book may be reproduced by any means, be they mechanical, or electronic process, or any recording devices, nor may the book be stored in a retrieval system, transmitted, or otherwise be copied for public or private use without prior written permission of the author.

Printed in the United States of America

Copyright page

Dedication

This book is dedicated to all who want emotional mastery over their lives.

Table of Content

Introduction	3
Chapter 1 - What caring what others think means	11
Chapter 2 - Why you care what others think	19
Chapter 3 - What you lose if you don't stop	31
Chapter 4 - What you gain if you stop	53
Chapter 5 - How to stop caring what others think of you	65
Chapter 6 - Every negative emotion holds a growth opportunity	83
Chapter 7 - Why children need to be taught how to not take things personally	119
Chapter 8 - How doing this self-work is making a powerful difference in the healing of our world	129
Chapter 9 - Can you imagine a world?	137
About the Author	141

How to not care what other people think

Introduction

Many of us are affected to varying degrees by how others perceive us. Many believe that the reason for this is that it benefits our socialization skills. This attribute, this part of us that cares about what others think, is supposed to make us control and shape our behavior to function together cohesively in a society. It is supposed to create a social norm that we can follow to live in harmony. It sets in place the acceptable:

manners, styles, etc. All of this is not necessarily a bad thing except if it in any way makes us lose your ability to be our best.

That feeling of wanting people to see you a certain way, or wanting people to think of you a certain way can often affect you to edit your decisions and actions away from what your heart may have genuinely wanted to do in the first place. The price you pay to live that way is often too high, but most people don't even notice that they are spending it.

*

Have you been told that you are too sensitive and that you need to get a thicker skin? Do others often have a lot of power to mess with you or put you down and take the wind right out of you? Do you often worry that you may have said something wrong or offended someone by mistake? Do you often worry that people may think badly of you and does that thought keep you up at night? These are some prominent examples of the adverse side effects that come from making what others think of you essential to your being.

*

I used to be a person who regularly lived my life in the ways that I described in the above paragraphs. Unlearning has been a journey all on its own. I still find myself being affected to a degree at times, especially in my fragile moments, but the awareness of it and knowing how to process it has been an excellent tool to have and I will be sharing with you what I have learnt in this book.

When I first decided to learn how not to let people's opinions hurt me so much, this is what happened. It was just the most blaring message from the Universe telling me, "Nancy, you are on the right track, stop caring what other people think of you."

"We take unnecessary things personally.

Almost everything we take personally is unnecessary".

It was in the thick of San Francisco's financial district traffic. It could take half an hour or more to go around only a few blocks. I was driving down Grant Avenue and I was waiting to take a right turn onto Geary Street in front of Neiman Marcus. It was two days before the new year began.

I saw a gray sports car in front of me, and I made a hand gesture for him to go ahead of me. The next thing that happened baffled me completely because the driver, a young man in his twenties or early thirties, angrily flipped me off. He had misunderstood entirely my intention or my waving him forward. I desperately tried to communicate that it was ok by waving him on again. To which he appeared to become even angrier and glared at me as he moved on.

I am not sure what he thought I meant, and I felt terrible for him, unable to explain through car windows that I was not saying what he thought I was saying. He was very offended, to say the least, for no reason at all. But of course, he didn't know that. I can be sure that he stayed fuming for a while after he drove ahead. Again, for no reason at all.

The funny thing was that at that moment, as he glared and drove forward, every fiber in my body wanted to feel offended by what he was doing. If I think about his gestures, I do still want to feel bad about it. I ended up laughing out loud just because of how funny the scene was and how appropriate that scene was for the very theme of "not taking things personally," the topic of a lesson that I happened to be studying at that time.

The driver of that car reacted the way he did because he misunderstood what I was saying.

I laughed instead of giving into feeling anger at his reaction because I was aware of the misunderstanding.

*

I wonder how many drivers misunderstand one another, just how this driver misunderstood my intention. Of course, there are times drivers intentionally make offensive gestures. Should the other driver, you or I, take it personally? What do you gain if you do take it personally?

What do you lose if you do? Those are fundamental questions to consider and answer for ourselves.

There are many other ways that we walk around, being offended by others. You do something special for someone, and they don't acknowledge you. Someone gives you a dirty look. A waiter takes orders from others before they take yours even though you got there first. Your friend or a loved one forgets your birthday. Someone calls you a derogatory name.

Do you have the right to feel offended? Of course, yes. Is it beneficial for you to get offended? No, never. I propose it does not help anyone, including and especially you, who is offended.

I am not advocating that you put up with abuse. You are an intelligent person, and you know that you cannot allow anyone to abuse you orally or otherwise.

I am talking about learning how to not waste your precious time, energy, and mind on what someone thinks about or does to you. I am talking about stopping doing things that take away from your becoming your whole fully realized person. I am talking about not letting anything or anyone get in the way of having a joyful life. I am talking about not letting anything stand in the way of you becoming empowered and a genuinely emotionally independent person.

"Care about people's approval, and you will always be their prisoner."

– Lao Tzu

Chapter 1 - What caring what others think means

The "caring" about what others think means that we take other people's actions to mean something about us.

It means that we think other people's words and actions represent who we are instead of seeing that it represents more closely who they are or at the least their understanding of who you are but not necessarily who you are.

*

When I say, "Stop caring what others think of you," I am not talking about being narcissistic, without empathy, belligerent, selfish, self-focused, uncaring, or blind to the needs of others. I am not advocating that you should be an anti-social human being.

*

When I say, "Stop caring about what other people think of you," I mean that you can learn how not to let other people's judgments, opinions and thoughts affect you in any way. You can become a person who practices being emotionally self-reliant in ways that benefit your ability to be your true and best self.

*

What I am talking about is becoming a person who can use the innate and natural abilities inside you to withstand people's opinions and know-how to see and decipher your truths.

*

What I am talking about is explicitly letting how you feel about yourself, your decisions, and your choices not be based on what others will think of you, while being someone who practices being self-driven with ease.

*

I think about what it must have been like for Ulysses Grant, who was once a distinguished military officer. Still, after leaving it behind, in the middle of the 19th century, he fell into deep and desperate poverty and had to do manual labor like carrying and selling coal, which barely fed his family. He was suffering.

He had been trying and failing to build financial stability for his family when he inherited a slave from his father-in-law, whom he could not keep nor sell, which would have brought him $1,000 (over $64,000 today). It was against his values. Selling the slave would have brought up his reputation amongst his peers, neighbors, and even his wife's family, who believed in owning and using slaves.

He would have been able to almost instantly erase the feeling of embarrassment at being inadequate and incapable of being a man who could support his wife and children.

He could have stopped doing labor like carrying and selling coals, which would have been well below a man of his education and community standing. Doing this work must have been embarrassing to him.

But he listened to his values and ethics, forgoing what he "looked like" to his community and peers.

He freed the man and continued to live in poverty. His inner compass controlled his decisions, not what he could look like to others.

Knowing how to live by your thoughts and values instead of how others see and judge you, no matter the situation, is what I am talking about in terms of not caring what others think of you and using that to control your decisions and actions.

*

I am also talking about you becoming a more consistently happy person so that your happiness is impacted by you and not others as the Greek philosopher, Epicurus, tried to teach us. I am talking about you being a person who cannot get distracted by others' opinions and thoughts about your correct life path, true self, and true spirit.

Epicurus devoted his life to teaching his students the concept of being happy no matter the condition, no matter what others thought of you, no matter what is happening around you, and even no matter what is happening to you. I am talking about being the master of your own emotions because you are indeed in charge of you.

*

In the coming chapters, I will explain how you and the rest of us got to this point of caring so much about what others think to the point of not living our best lives and how we can move out of that pattern and forward into our real lives.

"The eyes of others our prisons; their thoughts our cages."
— Virginia Woolf

Chapter 2 - Why you care what others think

One of the reasons why we care about what others think of us is because we were socialized and taught from an early age to do so to an extreme level.

Some may say that our caring about what others think of us is natural since most of us do it to varying degrees. But the reason why you can know that caring what others think is a learned behavior, a not necessarily healthy or profitable one, is that how we care depends on the culture you come from. If it was in our DNA, what we care about would be the same across all cultures.

*

Some cultures value speaking quietly and, if they talk too loudly, they are judged by their peers and feel ashamed of having done so.

Some cultures value individuality while other cultures value devotion to their group, so in one culture, you are judged if you don't show up as an individual, and in another culture, you are judged if you show up as an individual disregarding the group to whom you belong.

I grew up in a culture where if someone offered something to you, you were supposed to refuse it three times, and the giver was supposed to offer three times and, after three refusals, the receiver was to accept the gift, food, etc. If you defied that, it would be shameful, and you were judged and expected to feel embarrassed otherwise.

But if you behaved that way in America, you would be considered weak and passive and taught to feel embarrassed about being that way.

*

Some even believe this type of socialization is a good thing. It can have some positive outcomes in that the social pressure can encourage proactive behaviors like helping one's neighbor, coming to someone's rescue, etc., while preventing negative behaviors due to the same social need. Still, in both positive and negative cases, the socially pressured actions are not necessarily wholly dependable since it is not coming from the individual.

We may follow social pressures, but when that pressure is no longer there, we may not follow.

*

BF Skinner and other behaviorists influenced the furthering of socializing via opinions or feelings or judgments of others in powerful ways by discovering that we can use the emotional reactions to guide human beings.

Guiding human behaviors with positive or negative emotional rewards is as excellent and necessary as antibiotics are for bacterial infection. They work most of the time, but we also lose good bacteria while getting better.

As we guide and teach people to mold their behaviors appropriately according to outside stimuli and reactions, we lose out on individual self-reliant inner life practice. We will go into more of that in later chapters.

The question to ask is: does this way of living a life bring us consistent happiness and help us be the best version of ourselves? Does this really help us to be better humans for one another in our communities and the rest of the world? It is a worthwhile question to ponder, for our larger society's long-term mental health—the citizens of our planet Earth.

*

We learn to normalize caring what others think, and then we teach that way of life to our young, just as it was introduced to us. Just as our parents said to us, we tell our children things like, "What will your friends think if you did that? What will they say? What will they do? Will they be mad at you? Will they be disappointed? What will your father/mother say? What will your grandparents think/feel? Will they be proud of you? Will they still want to be your friend?" etc.

Those words are supposed to modify our behaviors, and they often do, but at what long-term cost? Saying things like that is very normal, but it does not mean it is healthy. Most people have a hard time forgiving themselves or others, but it does not mean that it is beneficial if you want to be as happy as you can be while being your best self.

This way of living does socialize us to a degree, to cooperate with one another in a community and our world. But at what cost?

We practice guessing and outguessing what others may think, may want, may need. We practice not our empathy toward others but what is considered acceptable and what may have been agreed upon by some abstract notion of the unsaid rules. We are all living life with our knowledge of others based on guesses, what we think we are supposed to think and want and do. This is an insidious, poisonous, unhealthy, and even silly way of living life.

*

Another contributor to our incessant caring what others think of us comes from the days of the saber-toothed tiger. We have genetic memories of surviving by keeping a watch on how others viewed us. If they found us acceptable to be a part of their group, it allowed us to survive as we were less likely to be caught and eaten by the saber-toothed tiger or any other dangerous animal. This is why being rejected by a group can feel so scary.

We can evolve out of this, however. We have also evolved our capacity to think. Our brain has grown along with our ability to assess and adopt to new environments.

*

Media in various forms set standards as to what and how we should care about and worry about meeting those set standards on their terms, and, if you come short of those standards, you are just not good enough.

There is a judgemental standard that most of us agree to abide by, having not a chance at arguing the validity. It is wholly taken up as the accepted, acceptable, and even beyond that, the way to be. I am talking about the styles, the material goods, the mannerisms, how we speak, and move, all of which are never bypassed through critical thinking of any kind. It goes straight to that basic desire from the days of cavemen to survive, which has turned into being admired and popular so that you can be more wealthy than others so that you can survive better than others, taking out all potential fear of being eaten by the saber-toothed tiger of the present moment: poverty.

We have become too busy trying to keep up with the idea of acceptability: acceptable weight, acceptable look, acceptable age, acceptable style, acceptable vehicles. All of these things are too quickly influenced by our incessant need to be good enough in other people's eyes, thoughts, opinions, etc.

*

Various forms of media perpetually feed the monster that is the need for acceptance. The "worrying about what others think of us," feeds into the profitability of media promoting the "acceptable ways to be." Their message is essentially: "If you do what we say you won't be eaten by the saber-toothed tiger, you won't be rejected."

*

If you were abused or neglected as a child, this problem is worse for you than others.

If you were abused or neglected as a child, your focus on what others think of you would be heightened. You would have learned to be hyper-vigilant in order to avoid the abuse and fear as much as possible by caring about what those abusers thought of you. Their opinions and judgments had a direct influence on what happened to you so you as an adult, if you have not processed what happened to you and healed yourself, are playing out that scenario of avoiding being hurt or avoiding being left alone and in danger.

If you were abused as a child, you might also assume the worst for yourself. You may imagine that people think the worst of you because you were prepared for the worst as a child. You may presume that people are thinking bad things about you and are constantly prepared for relationships not to work out. You probably let others decide or dictate where or how far the relationships go, presuming that they have opinions of you and you are stuck with those judgements, allowing what you think they think of you to dictate how things unfold.

*

If you are focused on your ego

I heard an artist say in an interview that one of the ingredients to success as an artist is a large ego. I disagree. Someone with a large ego having been successful does not imply that success is caused by the large ego itself. This particular artist, who was very successful and had a large ego, was also incredibly ambitious about giving a voice to the weak and the helpless. He seemed to want to give a voice to those who didn't have one. His music touched many hearts around the world because of this need of his to give voice to the poor. That is the very reason why I have always loved his music even though it took me a long time to like his vocal tones. On the other hand, it is likely that the chronic depression that ruled his life was caused by the large ego that could not be appeased unless he was on stage receiving all the attention that let him know that he was loved, he mattered, and that he was making an impact.

The ego's hunger never leads to anywhere good. Some of us are more prone to it than others. Some of us are more assertive with it than others. But if left unchecked, it can lead to the devastation of the person and relationships of all who relate to that person.

It is just too easy, especially if you have been mistreated in some way or have been taught that your ego, the artificial aggrandizing, even if you are not a chronic narcissist, can forget to really be in the present moment and experience the truth of the moments as it is constantly thinking, worrying, and acting on the need to prove its worthiness and specialness. As we move through life, being mindless as to how we habitually act around others or even within our own selves in the way we judge ourselves, we suffer unnecessarily and are prevented from reaching the best version of ourselves and living the best version of our lives.

As one of my favorite authors once said on stage, "Every moment, new reality." That means we don't have to continue repeating what has not worked even though we may have been trained by our own lives and our own environment. The way we have been encouraged to live is not fruitful for our true happiness.

"If being an egomaniac means I believe in what I do and in my art or music, then in that respect you can call me that… I believe in what I do, and I'll say it."

— John Lennon

Chapter 3 - What you lose if you don't stop

Lemuel destroyed his life and, along with it, the potential that at one time flowed unendingly. It seemed there was no one like him. In truth, there was no one like him.

Every film studio in town wanted him behind their cameras. He was the highest-paid and most coveted Steadicam operator in town. His slender and tightly muscular body worked in perfect concert with his eyes and mind for a look of his own to help him masterfully work the camera in ways that made movies filmed by him have a look that was like no other cameramen. Even the actors looked at him with appreciation, and the actresses showered him with attention so that he would remember them.

He made the actors, actresses, directors and producers, all look good. He was a fit 4th degree black belt Taekwondo practitioner with a square jaw and penetrating eyes. He was a good looking guy. He was charming and witty and could impress whoever he was focused on. He was acutely intelligent and perceptive. He noticed details like no one else, yet was also incredibly expansive in his creative visions like no one else. He was a godsend to any film producer, director, and everyone on set. He seemed to understand intuitively what the directors wanted and produce their heart's desire. He was every single one of those things and just one more thing. Ok, maybe few more things that were caused by his one thing.

His one thing was his irresistible need to have everyone impressed with him, to only think well of him and never see or think critically of anything he does, says, thinks, just anything at all to do with him.

When a new production assistant first arrived on the set, the first thing they were told was to never ever touch, move, clean, or do anything at all, or go anywhere near anything at all that may belong to the head cameraman. They were told that they would be fired on the spot if they did. There were many young PAs who forgot and, if they were lucky, they were fired. The unlucky ones walked away with either physical injury at the hands of Lamuel or psychological trauma also at the hands of Lamuel who could imprint a person with such a fear with just the right words that they would run out of the building and never return, even if they were not told that they were fired.

Lamuel learned his photography and film-making skills while training in the military where he was a skilled fighter with a photographic memory and extreme intelligence, with an amazing combination of talent and discipline in every pore of his body and mind. His superiors adored him. Yet, he would from time to time end up in solitary, having expertly used his knowledge of human body and its pain points, when angered by someone, to land his victim in a hospital with severe injury. Instead of feeling remorse, he would ask for a book and spend his time in jail, memorizing it. Once he memorized every word in an English Webster's dictionary, even though at that time, his skill in the English language was definitely not at an advanced level. Another time when he was put in solitary confinement, he memorized the Bible, even though he was a staunch atheist. He fascinated some around him and put fear in the hearts of others.

What crime did his victims commit that caused them to be beaten so badly and end up in hospitals, you ask? They dared to correct him, challenge him, disagree with him, or change something he meticulously set up. Everything he set up was meticulous. All of his meticulousness in his physical environment was supposed to protect him from his tremendous fear of losing his feeling of power that depended on everyone respecting him, everyone believing him, everyone following him, everyone being impressed with him, everyone thinking he was amazing, everyone thinking he was flawless in every single way. He let no one cross that need. Eventually, his superiors that adored him encouraged him to leave the military by getting him a job as a Steadicam operator on a film set. And they were not surprised when he flourished in that job.

He transported with him all of his need for everyone's obedience and violent temper when someone crossed those lines, but, in film studios, they could only fire so many PAs and anyone else who may have touched his equipment or his ideas and plans, who could be fired or sent to hospitals without the solitary confinement to put him away to punish him.

If his bosses would come to him and agree with someone's disagreements or correct him on his bad behavior, he would walk off sets, halting their film-making schedule, oftentimes, after breaking a thing or two on his way out.

The studio would have, by this time, learned just how they could get Lamuel to come back. They would come to his home, let him know how in the right he was. Of course, he was right, they would tell him.

He is a genius, and everyone knew it, they would add. Anyone who challenged his ideas was just jealous of all of his talents, they would add to assure the result that they sorely needed. "Fools," they would call those who offended Lamuel. The heads of studios coming to his home, begging him to please come back was the perfect elixir to calm Lamuel's fragile ego, fill his cup of needing to feel like the king that he needed to be, and he would go back to the studio proudly holding his head high.

After a decade of dealing with these yo-yo scenarios, all the studios in town decided to let go of their need to top each other by using the talented Lamuel. They wanted some sense of peace and decided to walk away from the turmoil and lose the genius.

Lamuel was entirely out of work, work that he loved doing more than anything. When he became unemployable, he took out all of his self-loathing on his adopted child and sometimes even on his wife.

Lamuel is an extreme example of what can unfold in the life of someone who cares too much about what others think of them. But we all know about those famous people who have lost lives that they loved because they needed to feed their egos at all costs.

All of these people who ended up losing everything are louder examples of what many of us do when we care too much about what others think of us, how they are judging us, and what we look like to the outside world.

Lamuel now lives with the idea of who he could have been, the stories of his past accomplishments when he was young, how perfect, and how much of a genius he was. He lives off stories that he makes up to tell his social circles and perhaps even makes himself believe his made-up stories to appease his broken heart. His Facebook avatar is a picture of himself in his uniform when he was an adored genius military man. He smiles in that photo. Both of his hands are on his hip in his hero pose. He is handsome, strong, and brilliant looking, as indeed he was. All that talent and brilliance kept safe in that vault of youth was never able to cross over to mature wisdom that required him to grow out of keeping his ego safe from judgment of others.

*

How Lamuel led his life is a cautionary tale for the rest of us. Your life experiences are so much better when you don't care what others think of you. I will go more deeply into that concept in the next chapter. But, for now, we need to go over in depth the many harms caused by caring about what others think of us.

There is a difference between caring about others and their wellbeing and caring about what they think of you, what image of you they hold in their minds: whether they are impressed with you or disappointed with you.

Caring about what others think of you turns you into a person who is less than you in so many ways. It also makes you far less happy than you could be. It makes you become easily affected by too many things to be as effective as you would like to be. It makes it difficult for you to have a truly joyous and fun life.

Caring about what others think of you gets in the way of your ability to live your best life. You end up wasting your time focusing on things that are not valuable and important for your life.

Firstly, you have no way of knowing what others are honestly thinking about. They may or may not be judging you as you are thinking or guessing that they are judging you. And if they are judging you in ways that you think that they are, based on how you interpreted what they said, based on how you interpreted how they said what they said, or based on how you interpreted the way they looked at you or didn't look at you, etc., if your interpretation is right, worrying about it gives you no fruit, or affects their decision to change their minds.

You have no way of controlling anyone's emotional behavior or any other behavior. As I just mentioned, you have no control over what they are going to think of you and, no matter how perfectly you behaved in front of them, they may still be judging you in the wrong way. They may misunderstand you, which many people do all the time anyway. You have no control over what people will think, so you are wasting your time by feeling bad and worrying about it. And all this is assuming that your assumption was right. And then again, you may be wrong and none of what you were thinking was happening in their minds.

Again, by focusing on what they are thinking, you are distracted from what you need to be doing, what you have control over, that which you need to focus on for your life. Thinking and worrying about what others think of you takes a lot of energy and time. It is a powerfully negative emotion, and it is incredibly draining.

In addition to being drained, when you are worrying about what others might be thinking of you, you will not be able to work on developing your authentic self because you will do what you think others want from you as you are worried about what others think of you. You will bypass your thoughts and opinions just to please those whose opinions you are worried about. If you are an extreme worrier, you will bend over backwards to do what would please them, so you will avoid whatever your true desire may be.

You will be constantly guessing what you think others want because your top goal is to please, and such guessing takes so much energy and emotional space that you will feel thrown off all the time. You will be robbed of thinking for yourself or making decisions based on what you truly desire.

You will not be thinking about what it is that you want because you will be prioritizing what others want from you, leaving you no room to think about what it is that you might want. And, even if you think about what you want, you would not be able to follow those feelings for fear of being disliked or being rejected by the people whose opinions of you, you care so much about.

*

You will constantly waste time feeling miserable because many people will be able to make you feel bad because they have the power to influence you. Since what they say and do affects you, they can simply do and say things that they know will affect you in the ways that they want you to be affected, and you are going to experience what it is that they designated for you to feel.

Many situations can make you feel bad since, again, your emotions are affected by people and events outside of your system of values, thoughts, and beliefs.

There are too many situations that can influence your feelings when you care about what others think of you. This means that the various people, events, and things will easily influence your emotional well-being.

*

You will misunderstand how things are in your environment.

It is difficult to see things with clarity since you are in the practice of seeing things based on your estimations of what others may be thinking and, with that influence, you are observing and making decisions about what is or isn't taking place.

You will misunderstand people constantly if you are under the influence of a certain way of thinking and you will get your feelings hurt easily since you will always presume to think the worst based on your own guesses about what other people are thinking.

It will keep you from growing and understanding if you are in the practice of thinking and worrying about what others are thinking of you as you will not have much time to think for yourself.

*

You will hurt relationships in your life without knowing that you are wrong.

You will be reacting to people and circumstances based on your beliefs about what happened, likely with hurt or angry feelings, without having full proof that your feelings are justified because you may have completely misunderstood what happened. In addition, even if you had assessed the situation correctly, it leaves you little room to gain a better understanding and so prevents you from engaging in healthier interactions that could lead to deeper relationships with others.

*

You will be small when you can be big and wise

You cannot gain proper wisdom when you are always taking things personally because you will be focused on you instead of understanding and learning. You will practice being small-minded and be minutely focused on things, preventing you and keeping you from truly learning about your truth.

*

You will not reach your potential.

You will be distracted and disjointed in your effort, diverted by the misery of feeling bad about others' opinions and thinking about how to fix how others feel and think about you.

Your reactions to others, whether they actually did things that you think or didn't do things that you think they did, either way, will impact your relationships with them, because of how you react to them.

You will not be able to access all of your potential because too much of your energy will be wasted on thinking about how others feel about you and having feelings about how others feel about you (good or bad).

Even if others' opinions are good, the good feelings that you experience can be destructive because you are becoming accustomed to someone else's feelings and behaviors, which you have no control over no matter how good you are. Even if you can affect their feelings to a certain degree by doing your 'best' (according to them), it is temporary and it robs you of your emotional liberty. If you allow someone else's opinion of you to affect you, you will always be drained of energy.

*

You will not be able to fully enjoy life

You will not be able to fully enjoy your life in the way that you truly deserve to or have the potential to because you will be living less well and more unpredictably, living according to expectations that are neither in your control nor reliable as they depend on random opinions. As I said, good or bad, depending on them makes your life unstable and out of your control.

*

You will not be able to see life as it really is.

When you are reliant upon others to affect your feelings and thinking, good or bad, if you care what others think of you, then your view of things will be affected by what you think others are thinking, or how others may judge you. It may even prevent you from being able to truly think for yourself and fully using your faculties to judge situations you come across.

When trying to make decisions while trying to affect the opinions, feelings, and thoughts of others, you cannot access your best logic, perception, or faculties. When you are under undue pressure, everything that you see is affected and skewed by confirmation bias.

*

You are emotionally vulnerable to the behavior of others, which you fundamentally have no control over. There is nothing wrong with being emotionally vulnerable, when it is about genuine feelings that you have toward others. However, when you are being artificially affected by issues that should not have anything to do with what you need to do with your life and what you need to be feeling about your life, it stops the true path of your life. It stops you from following your true path.

*

As you can see, caring about what others think of you often causes problems on an individual level.

If you habitually over personalize things that happen, you are essentially a raw emotional nerve always ready to be hurt. You will be prone to feel pain at the most innocent touch. You might even decide that the world is full of pain or that everyone hurts you. You will not always be able to sense correctly what is occurring because you trust distorted findings produced from a world view based on incorrect premises. This will result in the negative outcomes you expected, yet again confirming your distorted beliefs about the world.

For example: a man asks an attractive woman out on a date and she turns him down. If he takes it personally and decides it is an insult against him, he will take himself down an emotionally destructive path. His defensive mind may decide that all women are too picky, shallow and unloving.

Wearing that bitter negative attitude, he asks another woman out. He is turned down again. Most healthy and balanced women would sense his negative attitude and turn him down. He does everything he can to attract women, and when nothing works, he desperately flaunts his wealth. The one that finally says yes is a woman who has just as negative outlook on life, having decided that all men were not good for much other than what they could give her. When that relationship is over after he has lost a fortune on her and his belief that women are cold, heartless, and only want money is confirmed.

What would have happened if the same man had not taken the first woman's refusal personally, but had realized what it actually is: her own decision based on her personal feelings about him not being right for her? She may have been right or wrong, but her estimation of what he means to her reflects nothing about who he is. It is an observation that belongs to her and her alone.

*

Taking rejection is not easy for most people, but it does not have to be that way. It just takes learning how to look at rejection accurately and look at the facts. Not knowing how not to take these things personally costs too much.

Whether the rejection is about your love, your ideas, your work, your culture or your tribe of people, you must learn to depersonalize others' opinions or else you will suffer unnecessarily. Those hurt feelings will take your precious time, energy and focus away from your real life that you need so that you grow and prosper in your life's work.

*

Caring what others think causes problems in our community.

"What hurts the hive hurts the bee." — Marcus Aurelius

At a community level, a healthy, cooperative environment is difficult to create if the individuals in it are busy worrying about what everyone else is thinking about them. When everyone in the group is thinking this way about everyone else, it is difficult to ascertain when a real assessment is being made, ultimately leading affecting the quality coming out of the group. We all know how the leaders of organizations have failed miserably by being surrounded by "yes" people. When you look at healthy and successful leaders or a healthy and successful groups, there are always healthy number of truth seekers: people who willing to and are encouraged to express their truths as they see them.

*

And then, of course, we can see the obvious affects of caring what other people think in the way we live in and around our homes with our neighbors.

It has come to be normal for many people not to know who their neighbors are. Why is that? Perhaps we don't want to experience disliking them or them disliking us. We don't want to experience an unresolved conflict that we have experienced with others in the past.

If we don't know them, we won't take a chance at a bad experience. --- We are not learning about one another or practicing getting better at learning how to truly connect and we have become ok with that. We think it is normal to live amongst so many people never knowing who they are, never connecting with who they are, never experiencing who they are, never sharing who we are, and never gaining a sense of belonging. It has all become normal.

We do not question the strangeness of it. We all preemptively avoid one another to avoid their judgments of us and our potential judgment of them. We avoid practicing empathy as we avoid potential judgment. This creates a community full of lonely people. We miss out on experiencing the support and strength that can come from having a good, loving community.

This definitely hurts the community, even if you are used to how things are, it does not mean the hurting is not happening. It hurts the community in the following ways:

- Disconnection does not prevent crime but can permit and even encourage it.

- Disconnection causes feelings of danger that confirm or grow mistrust, suspicion, dislike, and lack of togetherness.

- It prevents people from being there for one another in deep, true ways.

- People are missing out on potential resources in one another: help, learning, being inspired, helping to heal, and helping to promote one another.

- People are missing out on growth as human beings.

- People are missing out on connections.

- People are missing out on happiness.

- People are missing out on the fullness of what life can be by staying behind the wall of fear… never growing our sympathetic muscles, empathetic muscles, communication muscles.

*

Caring about what others think of us as individuals in the end causes problems for our world.

Our whole world is made up of individuals. When each one of us is living in a limited state, not knowing how to love ourselves fully, constantly misunderstanding others, too often worried about what we look like to others, we live in a state of self-focus missing out on understanding others around ourselves because we are too busy trying to project an image, trying to figure out how to make people think a certain way… on a global scale we cannot expect to be making better, healthier choices.

How could we expect to have a peaceful world without hunger when so many of us are preoccupied with our own individual deficiencies and self-focus that drives us to being far less caring about what is best for the greater good? It is impossible.

"It's not what happens to you, but how you react to it that matters. When something happens, the only thing in your power is your attitude toward it; you can either accept it or resent it. Men are disturbed not by things, but by the view which they take of them."

--Epictetus

Chapter 4 - What you gain if you stop

When I was in fifth grade, I wrote a poem and entered a national poetry contest. I wrote about a man who inspired me throughout my childhood. King Sejong with the help of scholars who he nurtured for that purpose, invented the Korean written language. Before him Koreans used Chinese characters for their writing needs.

As a little girl, I was thankful to have the ability to write in my own language and could never get over the feat of that labor, how grand that seemed to me, that I could write down my thoughts because he, King Sejong, created it for my people.

As an adult, I gained a deeper appreciation for the man who was King Sejong. He was the son of a wealthy and ambitious king. He could have just simply lived the life of royalty. No one would have thought any less of him. He was intellectually curious and insatiable with regard to gaining knowledge, both as a child and as an adult. He dove into inventing, sun clocks, book printing machines due to his love for books, etc. He could have just indulged in those things that he loved doing and he did: inventions and reading. But he went deeper. He decided that it was not ok that only the wealthy and high class could read since Chinese written words were complex and cumbersome, not readily available for ordinary people.

What would have been normal for royalty was for him to care about his immediate needs? Those were the prevalent values and thoughts surrounding him. He could have had an easy life.

But he devoted his life, even losing his eyesight in the later part of his life, to the creation of a scholarly program that encouraged families to volunteer a son who had intellectual potential. If they did, he would financially support the son's family. The son would then dedicate his life to joining his work to invent Korean written language. He sent his scholars to the ends of the earth to research, study, learn and bring back knowledge that they could then use together, and finally invented the Korean written language. It is amazingly simple to learn, yet it meets the complex need to write any sound with vowels and consonants as well as a set system that everyone could use. It is a brilliant invention and he accomplished it all during his lifetime.

Most of the royal class advised against his endeavor for they did not want ordinary citizens to know how to read and write. There were many attempts on his life to try and prevent his endeavor. Many in the King's court thought him outrageous, fool-hearted (today someone might call him a 'bleeding heart liberal'). They tried to portray him as crazy foolish man who had lost his mind. He let none of those things stop him. He followed his heart and his mind to accomplish something that he felt was important for his people for the greater good. He was willing to risk even his own life to accomplish it. He persevered and accomplished it.

Koreans' lives would have been completely different today if King Sejong had been a person who was affected by the opinion, judgment, and thoughts of his peers. But because he followed his own thoughts and ignored others' opinions of him, he was able to accomplish something incredible: a written language for a whole culture.

Koreans gained from his disregard of what others thought, said, or even did to him. They even tried to take his life! He gained what he set out to and brought to life something so amazing by ignoring others' opinions of him.

*

Besides being able to accomplish your true life's work, stopping caring what others think leads to your best life because you will be far happier.

Your moods will not be erratically affected by what anyone else is doing or thinking or what they may be feeling or thinking because you will be relying solely on what you think and feel. You will have an even temperament because you use logic to think and feel, so you will make logical judgments instead of just thinking based your presumptions.

You are practicing emotional self-reliance, being your own judge of you according to your terms, values and ethics which helps you become self-trusting, which then makes your emotions more stable.

You will not waste time focusing on what is not important

Every time you spend time thinking, worrying or even wondering what someone else may be thinking about you, you waste your time. You have lost that time and you cannot get it back. You accomplish nothing while you are worrying about what someone else may be thinking about you. In fact the time that you spend doing eats away at your energy, your happiness, your productivity, your creativity, your genius, your ability to relate in genuine ways with others, you ability to relate with yourself in genuine way, and your ability to love and appreciate yourself for your true and genuine self. All this cuts away at your potential to be the best version of you.

By not worrying about what others are thinking about you, you can focus on what you are thinking about and what is important. And when you are focused on what is truly important to you, you are using your time and not wasting it.

*

By not caring what others are thinking, you will develop your authentic you.

When you are focused inward instead of focusing on how others are seeing you, you will be practicing listening to your thoughts and practice operating under the influence of your own thoughts.

*

By not caring what others are thinking, you will not be constantly wasting time feeling miserable.

So often people feel bad based on what others may be thinking of them or how someone may understand them to be, or what judgement someone may be making of them. You will be safe from all of that nonsense.

*

By not caring what others are thinking you will not actually misunderstand how things are in your environment. You will have a clearer outlook and be able to rely on evidence and logic to make judgments. You will be in the practice of doing it so you would be skilled at doing it. You will be able to really see life as it really is. You will not be encumbered with incorrect knowledge, incorrect ideas, and misunderstandings. You will be free to see life in the truest possible way.

*

By not caring what others think, you will not hurt relationships in your life without knowing that you are wrong. Since people often hurt their relationships casually with misunderstandings and far more often than most people realize by their own misunderstandings, you will be avoiding them and experience truer and deeper relationships. You will be gaining wisdom more regularly and be communicating better others, leading to the best relationships possible in terms of both intimate relationships and other relationships.

*

When you stop caring what others think, you will not be small when you can be big and wise.

Knowing how not to care what others think makes you see life beyond just your own image. You will grow your wisdom because you will be thinking beyond you and outside of you in an empathetic way.

*

When you stop caring what others think, you will reach your potential.

You will not be living a lie but seeking reality and experiencing a deeper truth and meaning that will affect everything you do.

*

When you stop caring what others think, you will be able to fully enjoy life.

You will be able to enjoy life to your full potential since you will not be drawing in bad feelings caused by worrying about what others are thinking of you.

*

Would you like to be more successful, happier, more joyful, more energetic, more powerful, more self-confident, more in touch with your own voice, more creative, and more at peace? If your answer is yes, then you are on the right path to work on gaining emotional mastery.

You will be more successful because you will have so much more energy and far less self-doubt to move forward with the endeavors of your life. You will be happier because you will not be suffering under the crippling feelings that you get when you let others' judgments affect you. You will be more joyful because you will see yourself and your world through a clearer lens, enabling you to see beauty and all the gifts that life has to offer you. You will have much more energy because you will not be robbed of it by suffering unnecessarily. You will be more powerful because you will allow yourself to be more powerful as you are no longer under the weight of negative judgements or what you may have thought to be negative judgments from others. You will be more in touch with your own voice and experience your best creativity because you will be free to experience those things. Finally, you will be more at peace because you will be free of all the garbage thoughts hanging around in your mind. You will be free to just be.

When you learn how to depersonalize others' thoughts of you, you become free of the need to impress others, helping you to become an authentic person of your own making. When you do that, other people will feel more at ease with you and you, just being your authentic you, will be cause joy for others around you without putting in any effort.

In this form, you are helping to create a better world, just being you, effortlessly.

"You have no responsibility to live up to what other people think you ought to accomplish. I have no responsibility to be like they expect me to be. It's their mistake, not my failing."

— Richard P. Feynman

Chapter 5 - How to stop caring what others think of you

A great stoic philosopher, Marcus Aurelius's life embodies the essence of how not to care what others think of you. He's a great example of a person who lived his daily life focusing inward: doing, thinking, deciding, acting, and feeling what he deemed aligned with his values of being a good man. For him this meant a man that would please the gods, but really it meant to satisfy the moral values that he held himself to practice daily.

He practiced not worrying about what his image looked like or what others were saying about him. Instead, he worried about living each of his days doing what he deemed morally right, being a good person according to his own assessment. He did his very best to live that way by evaluating his actions, reactions, decisions, even his own emotional state, on a daily basis, staying alert to being his best self.

Although we are not emperors, we do all have responsibility to be the best version of ourselves so that we can first make a powerfully positive impact in our own lives and then powerfully positively impact the lives of all who we love and in our world. Follow the steps that you can take to live your life in highly positive way as Emperor Marcus Aurelius did with his.

Your Foundation:

Do self-work

- Practice unconditional self-love
- Practice unconditional self-acceptance
- Meditate daily
- Practice excellent self-care (health of your body affects your mind and your spirit)

- Practice honoring your boundaries

Practice living your values to remember that living according to your values is what you are aiming to do (i.e. it's not about impressing others)

- Every morning write out what values you will practice
- Every night look over your list to check off your success

Know: What is your work? How will you make your positive difference in the world?

*

Things to start practicing every day to build the habit of not caring.

- First thing in the morning write out what you will do to be the person that you want to be and to not be who you do not want to be.
- Before going to bed, look at your list to see if you have met your daily goals of who you want to be. If you met your goals, you have lived your day according to your

own values. Your daily goal is to live according to your goals and values.

*

Things to stop practicing that will help you not care what others think but become an emotionally self reliant person who focuses on your own values and not what others think of you:

- Don't brag. While doing it might make you feel good in the moment, you are internally telling yourself that you are not enough. It is a powerful message. If you have to boost your self-image to others, you are feeling not good enough. Look at it. Learn to stop doing it for good.
- Don't try to impress others. This also accomplishes the same thing as above. By doing it, you are believing something about you is not enough and you are also reinforcing that message. It does not matter how others see you and you don't clearly know how others see you. Just be, observe, and experience the moments. Be joyful just as you are.
- Don't give to gain affection or attention. This also accomplishes the same as the above. You are saying to yourself that you are not enough. You are enough. It

does not matter what someone may or may not think about you. Just be.
- Don't try to get attention. Get to know others deeply
- Stop seeking validation from others. What others think of you is meaningless. People often misjudge or judge based on seeing things through their own worldview and the state of their own lives. Whether their judgement is good or bad, you have to learn to base your ideas about your actions and thoughts on your own decisions and assessments.
- Stop needing to feel good about yourself. Accept who and how you are, which does not mean stopping your growth. Simply accept your flaws or imperfections and who you are right now as you are. Aim to just be, not good or bad.
- Don't be a victim. (emotional state of self-pity/victim mentality) The self-help era has done a lot of good. But it also trained you to dwell too much in the past and sometimes even identifying yourself as a victim. You have been victimized by something or someone. Everyone has. Heal and move on so that you can be whole now and in your future.
- Don't be tied to your ego.

- "There is no self." — Alan Watts A powerful way to become truly insulated from getting hurt by someone's negative words or judgments of you is to practice moving beyond your ego. It is very mundane and boring to be so attached to one's ego. When you are in the midst of being in that mode, you are being nothing but a self-absorbed person who needs a fresh perspective and a wake-up from sleeping through life. It is a type of life that makes it hard to really see what is going on because you're too closely focused on a very small point of life. When you allow yourself to expand and to be a part of the bigger picture of life as you truly deserve that's when life become so much more enjoyable as you are seeing so much more of it than you did before.
- Now you can see the bigger picture, your focus then becomes making a positive difference in your world. It becomes not about who you are but what you are doing. If who you becomes unimportant to you, then no one can threaten it. You would then be in the purest state that you can be in. Your life then becomes about truth,

what you are doing to contribute using your voice.

*

When hurtful things come up

Question logically if the meaning that you attach or what you think took place actually took place in the way that you are thinking. For example, some stranger sees you on the bus and exclaims, "you are fat." It would be reasonable for you to feel offended. You can be offended if you want to be. But what if that person who said it actually did not mean to offend you? What if in her culture, "fat" is a symbol of wealth, health and attractiveness?

That's exactly what happened to me when I was a young mom with my son riding on a bus when a young woman around my own age came up to me and said, "your son is fat." I was so offended that I could not forget it and later that even mentioned it to a friend of mine. My friend asked me if the young woman was an African American. When I said, "Yes," she said, "it was a compliment." She was telling you that your boy looks good.

Learn the difference between what you have control over and what you don't

Even if what took place did take place, in the way that you viewed it (i.e., the meaning that they intended is what you truly understood them to have said) what they did, said, and thought is not under your control. There is nothing that you can do about that so feeling bad about it is a wasted effort on your part. I y "wasted effort" because, even though it may seem involuntary, it really is not. When you are feeling bad about things of this nature, you, in some way, though illogically, are feeling bad in an effort to control the outcome. It's like watching the news constantly thinking that just by watching and keeping an eye on it you somehow have control over what is happening in the world. You are feeling bad and are trying to keep track of that event in order to control it, but, as you know, it does not work.

If we were to apply this to the story, I just discussed, about the young woman who said my son was "fat." Even though she actually meant it as a compliment, let's for argument sake say that she said it to be mean. She actually meant the word, "fat," in the way that many people say it, a derogatory negative putdown: an insult.

There are so many layers to looking at this situation.

- Was she right?
- If she was right, what does that really mean?
- If she was wrong, why does it matter what she said or says?

- If what she said matters in some way, to your reputation perhaps, is there anything that you can do about it?

- If there is anything that you can do to prevent the bad reputation from spreading, you can do the best that you can, using all the power and resources that you have, if this reputation is even worth doing something about. Most of the time the words that people say have very little affect on your life. But, let's say that they do have an affect, then you can do everything within your power not to further the energy drain and harmful emotional effects on yourself. You have to let it all go because the rest is out of your control and it is a silly and unintelligent thing to waste more of your energy working on it, thinking about it, mulling over it and feeling bad about it.

- In addition, if what a person says had no bearing on your business, their words actually have no physical effect on you, which is mostly the case, then what does it matter what a person says? The only power they have over you in this case is the power that you give to that person's word. They can say anything, make any sounds, or even expressions at you that they want, but it doesn't change your life at all. Not at all, except for what you agree to change based on what you decide to do with their words, which leads me to my next point.

- Learn that it's not what happens but the meaning that you put on what happens that has power over you.

- This means that whatever takes place, it is the meaning that you place on the event which then influences how you react to the situation emotionally and in other ways. For instance, it was the meaning that I placed on the young woman's word, "fat", that made me stop my fun and potential beautiful connection with a new person. I missed out on getting to know her all together even though I at first liked her as she seemed to like me. I then walked around the rest of the afternoon feeling offended, carrying around the negative feeling, which could not have been good for me in any way, shape, or form.

- What if I had decided that what she said didn't matter to me, that even if she said it with a negative intention, that it is about her and who she is and nothing to do with me and my son.

- Next, I could have thought that I have truly no idea what she means by what she said. We were having a fun time up to that point. I could have given her the benefit of the doubt and paused my judgments as to what meaning her words held. I could have done that and continued connecting with her, having fun talking and laughing and saved myself the unnecessary suffering that happened the rest of the day.

- I then would find out that she actually meant well by it. And that is another thought that I could have had. I could have placed a different meaning on her words, which would have meant that I could have gotten to know the young woman and, perhaps, gotten to know her on a deeper level and even learned something more about life from her.

*

"When you wake up in the morning, tell yourself: the people I deal with today will be meddling, ungrateful, arrogant, dishonest, jealous and surly. They are like this because they can't tell good from evil. But I have seen the beauty of good, and the ugliness of evil, and have recognized that the wrongdoer has a nature related to my own — not of the same blood and birth, but the same mind, and possessing a share of the divine. And so none of them can hurt me. No one can implicate me in ugliness. Nor can I feel angry at my relative, or hate him. We were born to work together like feet, hands and eyes, like the two rows of teeth, upper and lower. To obstruct each other is unnatural. To feel anger at someone, to turn your back on him: these are unnatural."

— Marcus Aurelius

Next, decide that human beings (ourselves included) are imperfect so they/we will inevitably say or do things that are unkind, thoughtless, selfish, malicious, jealous, foolish, untrue, unfair, and even unjust. This is the human condition. And we are all a part of this human condition. We are a part of it, as Marcus Aurelius has said, in a way that makes us all partners in crime. We are all responsible for it directly or indirectly, spiritually, and in every way that exists in our seen and unseen realm. Since we all belong to a greater whole, to accept and love one another flaws and all, in turn, is giving love to our separate and whole selves.

It makes it difficult to sit around feeling victimized or unjustly handled by someone when you see, as Marcus Aurelius reminded himself to see others in his journal (*Meditations*), that we all belong to one another and that when we do make mistakes we really truly did not or do not know what we were doing or are doing. Those words, of course, were echoed by Christ on the cross, "Forgive them father, for they know not what they do."

Putting aside the spiritual aspects to all of this, let's address a very practical issue. If someone calls you a name or puts you down by telling you that you are not good enough or, worse, that you are terrible in some way. You are hurt by what they said to you. That is the norm. Everyone can understand that. You wish with all your heart that people would simply not do that.

I know this feeling because I did that for years. I wished for it. I yelled at people for it. I begged people for it. I instructed people for it. I cried at people for it. I ran away from people for it. I tried everything that I possibly could to stop people from doing that to me.

Nothing, none of those things that I tried, worked. The truth is that none of us has the power to control anyone. None of us has the power to stop anyone from doing anything or saying anything that they want to do or say. Nor should we. We may have some influence but trying to influence, investing time into influencing, in turn, robs us, or at the very least takes away from the time that we must invest and we could invest in living our best lives and being the best human beings that we can be, as the Emperor Marcus Aurelius did almost 2000 years ago.

Here are the facts:

- You have no control over what they do or say.

- The words and their intention belong to them, not you.

- They are feeling whatever it is they are feeling and they are opening their mouths to make noise that they think represents their feelings. Their feelings and words are not yours.

- Their words and actions have nothing to do with you. It is not about you and it is not personal (even if they think it and you think it as well).

- Their willingness to put anyone down reflects on who they are, not on you.

- Their words and actions represent who they are, not you. If they yelled, "You are a river." Does that mean you are a river? Would you be offended and hurt, if they called you a river? It does not mean that you are a river, but it does mean that they might be delusional or, at the very least, that they need new glasses.

- If you are feeling hurt, you are placing value on their words. If you are placing value on their words, you are accepting a terrible gift. Do not accept what they are giving you. You need to get yourself a new mirror (your internal evaluation system, your sense of yourself, your value of you), to see and know that you are not a "river" but a human being of value and worthy of love, a person who is enough just as you are.

- If you allow their words to hurt you, it is like taking a stick that someone tried to hit you with off of their hands and then you hitting yourself the way they wanted to hit you. The stick is in their hands. The words are in their minds. Leave the words in their minds and walk away free. Do not grab the words and hit yourself with them by taking it on. The words belong to them. Let them have it. You don't need them. You don't want them.

- Sometimes, you are hurt by what someone says, because you believe their words on some level. If you work on how you feel about yourself and find your own truth or improve what you want to improve, you will not be vulnerable to getting hurt by someone saying those things to you. I will go over this with you in more depth in the next chapter.

"Be who you are and say what you feel, because those who mind don't matter and those who matter don't mind."

— Dr. Seuss

Chapter 6 - Every negative emotion holds a growth opportunity

---

You learn about yourself and you learn how to be emotionally independent. You gain emotional skills.

*

All my adult life I fought the pain. I did everything that I could to avoid it. All my attempts to fight and avoid it always worked like a boomerang that would bring me back to it except it came back stronger and for longer.

What I finally figured out was that I needed to turn squarely toward the things that were painful, face them, study them, learn about myself through that process and heal parts of my life.

In the end I grew, became stronger, and gained emotional mastery and emotional independence in ways that I could only have dreamt of. This very thing is what I want you to gain because gaining that has been and continues to be one of the most empowering discoveries of my life and I know that it will be that way for you as well.

There is a lot that you can learn from your hurt feelings, offended moments, and even your angry moments. Instead of just indulging in those negative emotions or even judging yourself for failing to know how to deal with them in the new ways that you have been learning this book, become an investigator of your emotions.

This way you will gain not only knowledge about yourself, but also emotional mastery by investigating, understanding, learning, gaining new insights, gaining life skills, and even gaining great wisdom.

*

As you begin implementing this new practice into your emotional life, you will run into situations that will challenge your skills. You will feel affected by someone's words or behavior. Don't feel bad. You are not failing. You are noticing it.

This means you are already well on your way. When you feel it, it is an opportunity for you to learn something new about yourself.

*

Just about every time a bad feeling comes up for you, you are unearthing something that you have needed to address. These moments remind you of what has not yet healed completely. These moments are also your great opportunity to grow and strengthen yourself emotionally.

*

Let's take a look at what some of those growth opportunities may look like and how you could react to them so that you can use them to make yourself even more powerful:

*

Someone treats you as if you are their inferior. If you feel offended by how they are looking at you: treating you if they are above you and you are beneath them, treating you as if you are less than them, less worthy than they are in some way, this is a great opportunity for you to learn and grow.

This is why. If you are feeling bad because they are looking at you as if you are their inferior, if you feel that they are looking down at you, then it is because somewhere deep down, you agree with what you believe to be their opinion of you.

*

If you are clear about who you are and what you are about, then whatever thoughts others have about you will not affect your opinion of yourself. You will simply disagree. Imagine if a child came up to you and insisted that you are a Santa Claus. You know that you are not Santa Claus so what they think will not make you feel offended.

*

Another example would be if you had been struggling to put on weight all of your life. You have always been too thin. If someone said you are fat and laughed out loud claiming it, you would look at them and wonder what might be wrong with their eyesight but you would not be offended.

While at the same time, if you are even just a little overweight and you have always struggled to be slimmer and someone called you "fat," you would be greatly offended because you have always been insecure about your body image, specifically concerned about being fat.

If someone were to tell you that you are stupid, but all your life you have known that you are intelligent and you are happy with your level of intelligence, you would simply just know that they are wrong. However, if you are insecure about your intelligence, someone thinking that you are less than intelligent will offend you.

*

Here's the thing, every one of those things that offend you are things that you need to work on within yourself. You either need to come to accept yourself for exactly who you are and, in some cases, you can also work on improving those areas of your life, not to feel better about yourself but so that you can enrich your life with more knowledge and wisdom.

*

There is also another way that makes you feel negative emotions that is not necessarily about feeling offended by others but is about judging others. It indirectly affects you in that it causes you to care what others think of you.

If you find yourself feeling superior to others, and you are judging others to be inferior to you in whatever way, that feeling is still about caring about what others think of you and being affected by what others think of you. It's just the other side of the coin.

Check your emotional actions and notice when you look at someone and just simply don't like them or feel irritated by the way they are.

What kind of people do you look at and think negative things about them? Are you bothered when someone seems sloppy, undereducated, unhealthy or poor, etc? If you are feeling that way, you are judging them and feeling superior to them. If you are feeling those superior feelings, it is time to investigate why you feel that way about those people.

Often when we dislike certain things about people, especially when they bring up strong feelings, it deeply reflects our own fears about having those characteristics. Investigate why you fear having those characteristics. Perhaps you were taught that those characteristics are shameful or weak or unattractive and, whatever you do, you must never have those characteristics.

The thing to realize is that when you can see those people and practice unconditionally loving them, that they are a part of you and that you are a part of them, they simply represent another soul doing their very best to be and live their lives to their utmost potential.

Think of someone that you criticise, or just don't like. Think about what it is that you don't like. Is it the way they speak? Is it the way they look? Is it the way they carry themselves? Is it their success level? Whatever it is about them that you don't like, ask yourself first of all: do you fear you may have any of those characteristics, even sometimes?

Then go back to that person and picture them in your mind being or doing something that bothers you. Try to feel compassion for them. Keep doing it in your mind until you feel nothing but warmth and unconditional acceptance for that person. Doing this exercise will firstly help you to unconditionally accept another human being, your fellow human being on this earth.

It will also help you become free of the irritation that you feel whenever you come in contact with them in any way. And then it will help you become a more powerfully and unconditionally self-accepting person who will have lost that particular judgement of yourself that you may have so feared. This will help you be free of others who may judge you using those criteria, allowing them not to bother you if and when they ever judge you in that way.

*

Feeling better than others is a powerfully dangerous trap, no matter who it is that we are feeling better than. It is just too easy. It is emotional candy for times when we feel less than good about ourselves. But, like candy, it tastes good for a minute and then goes on to create havoc on our system without us really knowing that it is doing that.

When we feel better than someone else, it masks a painful area of our lives. By masking that area, we are allowing the infection (insecurity) to fester and grow only to blow up in our lives in other ways. In addition, by not facing the insecurity, we are not resolving, growing, and improving in some way, either in how we feel about ourselves or how we are doing in things that are important to us and our life's work.

Feeling better than others can be contagious, especially with all the comparisons people make either it is about individuals or groups (racism). There's always laughter, fun, connections, and encouragement, normalizing behavior that is both unhealthy and destructive because everyone is doing it. The infection continues to spreads and takes a hold in our systems and in the systems of our society.

While all that is going on, it isn't only the society and others that we harm, but ourselves. As we prevent our true healing of our insecurities, we do not improve, we do not heal and we do not become stronger as individuals.

It is only by seeing the feelings of superiority as an opportunity (a sign or a symptom of the problem) to notice them and then to address it, investigate it, and resolve it, that we grow, heal, and strengthen ourselves.

For example, if you see someone a bit overweight and frumpy. You make a calculation of their looks and compare it to yours and feel better about yourself because you are better in those areas of life than that person. If you are feeling that way, then you are feeling insecure about your body. Even if you are in tip-top shape and you know that you are, you have not mastered your feelings about yourself. You have your sense of worth wrapped up in how fit you are and your sense of worth should not be tied to how fit you are. How fit you are is something that you can choose. It is certainly a healthy choice and this choice can also benefits your mind as well as your physical body.

So, when you see yourself feeling better than someone else because of your fitness level, you know that you have to work on knowing that you are lovable and worthy of love unimpeded by your level of fitness or how you look. Doing this work is incredibly important because if your sense of worth is dependent on your fitness and how you look, you stand on fragile ground in your sense of worth.

The answer to this is — it is going to sound extremely simple but it is extremely powerful — to do self-love exercises every day and every moment that you have free. Sit down in a quiet space, go inside yourself, and give yourself unconditional love. Tell yourself the pure self that you can feel and see in your mind's eye, that self, you tell them that there is nothing you need to do, you are loved, purely loved, by you. Feel the feelings as you tell yourself that you love you. And then love you. Tell yourself you love you as many times as you can as often as you can while feeling the love for yourself, just like when you say it to someone else that you love.

***Doing the exercise is very helpful during emotionally tough moments as well. When you feel rejected, hurt, depressed, worried, insecure, be in a safe place where you can go inward and just tell yourself with all your heart that you love you, again and again, passionately. Watch how changed you feel. It is powerful.

It is when you see that you are not better than anyone else, no matter the circumstance and choices and actions that other people are engaging in, that you know you have arrived.

When you are in a place of knowing clearly that no one is better than anyone, you will not feel offended by someone acting superior to you. And when someone treats you that way you will know how to respond correctly, not from a place of hurt or injury, but compassion and empathy for their insecurity. They, who are treating you that way, need to feel superior to you to mask their own sense of inferiority.

*

Road rage, when you are met with it, is a wonderful opportunity to learn fantastic emotional/life skills.

When a driver on the road behaves rudely, most of us, unless you are the utmost evolved and peaceful monk, feel offended. Even if you are a person who customarily flies off the handle at sight of road rage, you still most likely feel offended.

Have you ever just gone into anger mode and perhaps even tried to fight back in your own way by yelling out the window, making hand gestures or at the very least just yelled angry words to yourself in your car? If you have, do you remember how you felt during that time? Was it a good feeling? Did you feel happy during your anger? Did you feel smart and creative? Did you feel healthy and strong? Did you feel like you were being the best version of you?

I am going to guess that you did not feel any of those good feelings.

In fact, what you would have experienced during and after are a whole bunch of negative feelings. You perhaps even tired from the exertion and in the aftermath of the stress.

So, why would you have done that? Why would you have wasted your time and invested in an energy-draining experience? We are taught this and we are also taught the triggers as well. Growing up we watch adults participate in these behaviors. We also watch and feel their feelings as we empathize with them. After years of this experience, our emotional selves learn the outer manifestations of behaviors, the responses to the stimulus (the road rage or rude behaviors of other drivers), and our emotions get triggered and what we watched our parents do gets practiced effortlessly.

Questioning those emotional reactions and the emotional triggers that those events cause is not our norm as we think that it is just normal to have those emotional reactions. Well, it actually is true, it is quite normal. But this normal is not healthy like many other norms. And, like so many unhealthy norms, this normal is easily unlearned and it is silly to NOT unlearn it since it is also harmful to our lives.

It is harmful to our emotional well-being. And it is also harmful to our physical well-being. It is harmful to our emotional well-being because it is stressful, produces cortisol (stress hormone), which puts us in fight or flight mode, stunts creative thinking, and stunts logical thinking. If it is practiced enough, you can become someone who is quick to anger because anger produces addictive hormones that become reliant on just like with addictive drugs. This makes you become increasingly easy to anger and that itself has so many more side effects than just your own unhappiness, including unhealthy and disconnected relationships.

It is also bad for our bodies since, as I stated earlier, it produces cortisol which can make you gain unwanted weight. But that is only a small side effect compared to the negative effects on your health that you experience because, when you are in a negative state of mind, it affects your immune system in a powerful way. So many studies have been done now that make it obvious that our emotional states are powerful influences on our bodies either helping us to be vibrant, healthy, and youthful or to be tired, sickly, and age more quickly.

So, what you can do instead of experiencing all of those terrible things? Use that moment, when it occurs, to learn something powerful.

What someone else does, thinks, says, acts out, reacts, or feels does not represent the truth of the situation. Nothing that anyone else thinks means anything about you. This concept is sometimes a hard one to register in our hearts. When someone does something or says something to us, it is easy to internalize. There are, of course, many good reasons for that. One of them is that it is our natural survival instinct. But after the initial feelings are triggered, we can use our logic to deduce a different meaning, changing our experience to a non-harmful one.

*

"Choose not to be harmed—and you won't feel harmed. Don't feel harmed—and you haven't been."

— Marcus Aurelius

The Stoic philosophers have taught us that it is the very power that you give yourself, you already have. You have the power to allow yourself to drive your focus onto things that are truly important and worthy of your chosen experience.

A complete stranger is having a bad day maybe they just lost their job, maybe they are late for picking up their child from school or maybe they really have to go to the bathroom. Whatever the scenario that is unfolding inside them is what is making them act the way they do or say the things that they say.

You have nothing to prove to them. Will trying and proving something to them say something about you? Why would you want to prove anything to someone who does not really care to know anything about you? Also, why do you even need to prove anything to someone who never even misunderstood you or who even knows you? It is like trying to solve a math equation that does not exist anywhere. It would simply be a waste of your very precious time.

And, of course, the same reason as to why you don't have to take anything that anyone else, even those who are not strangers to you, personally applies.

The truth is that when you find yourself feeling offended by someone's actions like road rage, you can remind yourself that you are susceptible to using the old ways of thinking. While you have been working on not letting people's opinions and thoughts bother you, you have more practicing to do. And, in fact, you can use road rage situations powerfully to your advantage because it is so easy to conclude logically that the person's actions were not personal, since they are a stranger. It was all about them, but you felt offended.

This then can be applied to a person who does know you, or a person that you know (since not everyone who you know knows you that well). Even those who may know you more than others in your life do, when they act in ways or say things in ways that you find offensive or hurt your feelings, it is never about you, it is always about them, truly. Learning this is a powerful life skill.

*

When someone disagrees with you or challenges your beliefs, and you find yourself feeling offended, hurt, or even angry, it is a great learning moment for you.

It can be difficult, especially when it is a moral issue. If you feel frustrated to witness someone coming to a conclusion based on a false premise that might result in a negative outcome for your community, your country, and your world, anger is understandable.

We all feel this. We all experience frustration at seeing someone being gullible and clutching to their beliefs even though you know that what they believe is false.

You are a logical person. You have done your share of study on the various topics. You may even have obsessively studied this topic.

You find it mind-boggling that intelligent people can buy into what you consider baloney. You feel all this and more. It is so frustrating and offensive to you that they do not take your ideas and thoughts and even your hard work on this topic into consideration. You wish that they would give your ideas and thoughts a chance, just one chance, that is all that you are asking but they won't. They keep to their opinion and will not budge as if none of your ideas, knowledge or experiences count at all.

Let me tell you about the term, "confirmation bias." Confirmation bias plays strongly in the lives of those who hold so tightly to their beliefs. Confirmation bias is about the act of choosing data that agrees with the person's previously held belief and ignoring the data that disagrees with their already held belief.

That's why when you try and present your ideas, your facts, and the data that you think would make them change their mind, you feel frustrated and roadblocked when they just do not seem to hear you. Even if they seem to hear you, the ideas that you present and even the data that you present just bounces right off of them.

You sit there thinking, "How is that possible, these are the facts. How is it that you do not see what I am talking about?" But they don't see what you are talking about because when the data that you present goes into their ears and into their brains, the data doesn't jive with their existing beliefs so the data simply get rejected.

The thing to remember is that they are not trying to contradict you, they just are in a way defensively holding onto their existing beliefs because their brains actually feel good when they do that.

The scary thing is that that the same confirmation bias that is influencing them is doing the same thing in your brain. So, we think we are logical, fact-based, and truth-seeking human beings but we are also under the influence of confirmation bias. Our brains also like to reject the data that do not agree with our existing beliefs.

Even if you consider yourself a pretty self-aware person, it is something to consider. We must question our own biases even if others do not.

*

I have certainly experienced times where someone would just disregard something that I said. I would feel insulted at not being taken seriously even with my knowledge and experience. I have felt that way especially with people who I know to be less experienced than I am.

If you are experiencing this sort of feeling, it is an opportunity to look into why you feel the way you do. I realize that the feeling is pretty normal and many, maybe even all of us, go through the same thing. But, as I have said in another part of this book, what is normal is not always a good thing and, sometimes, it really is a bad thing.

The reason why you are feeling offended is that somehow someone not taking you seriously means that an offense has been done against you. There are so many possible scenarios as to why the person is not taking your ideas seriously. It could also be that they have a habit of simply ignoring everyone because they are egotistical. They might just have their own confirmation bias, as all humans beings naturally do have, and they are having a difficult time letting go of that. Even if you may disagree with their beliefs, you also cannot blame them for simply just being humans.

If you, on the other hand, feel insulted or angry that someone challenges your thoughts, then it is imperative that you take a look at your own sense of self. If someone verbalizing their differing opinions makes you feel defensive and you find yourself speaking or acting angrily, you have to pause and investigate where your feelings are coming from.

As you have the right to form opinions based on your own observations, others around you have the same right. You have the right to form a wrong opinion as they have the right to do the same.

If you find yourself feeling as if they are judging your intelligence, this is a very good opportunity for you to learn that you are not on solid ground with regard to your level of intelligence. You need to do some self-reflection, self-acceptance, and self-evaluation about that issue. It is important to come to terms with your own sense of intelligence,

*

And here is the thing. It is good to be curious and hunger to learn more. That is an excellent state to be in, to help you to become a more informed person and the best thinker that you can be. In terms of questioning or judging the level of your intelligence, you can stop doing that right now. No matter how smart you are, how high your IQ is, you are acceptable and perfect just as you are. I am not saying don't grow or learn because, when you stop learning and growing, you become boring to yourself. Human beings naturally love learning and growing. Our brains love it. It is like candy to our brains. What I am talking about is judging the level of your intelligence and judging yourself based on that. You may feel good about the fact that you have a high IQ. You might feel bad that your IQ is average or lower. Both of those feelings, good and bad, are a waste of your time and not really good for you. Let go of feeling either. Just be. Just grow. Just enjoy life and be your very best.

*

When someone puts you down in some way and you feel hurt or offended, it is another good opportunity for you to grow. If you feel bad and what they say makes you feel like what they said about you, that means that there is a part of you that agrees with the sentiment or idea.

If someone tells you that you are a terrible chef and you are a chef by profession and are confident in your chef skills, then what they say would not make you doubt yourself. But, if there is any doubt in you at all about your abilities as a chef, then you will be thrown off and experience doubt. If you are following your work ethics, doing your very best and still feel insecure, you need to work on knowing your worth as well as starting to practice doing your very best then letting it go once you are done. Know that is your job to do your best, then let it go.

If someone calls you names like, "stupid, loser, fat," the first thing that you must see is that the name-calling itself is bad behavior and the behavior belongs to the person saying those words. When people are putting you down, they are in a destructive mode and lashing out. It is all about who they are, no matter what excuse they give for their actions, it is them who are having the trouble with their emotions, and are lashing out hoping to feel better. It does not work.

The next thing to do is to move through it fearlessly. Don't get defensive. You don't need to defend it. Nothing is happening to you other than what you allow to happen to you. You can just let their throwaway comments go wherever. You don't have to let any of it land on you. Just be a peaceful observer. It's like you are just looking at it pass in front of you, but not reaching out to connect, touch, or feel it. You don't even have to understand it.

If you feel bad, is because someone is trying to attack your ego. Because they assume, that like them, your ego would be affected. But you are not your ego. Don't be afraid. You can just sit and witness it. Their words cannot hurt you unless you decide to let them hurt you. It really is up to you.

Another thing to do is to examine those words and see why you feel bad. Do you feel stupid? Do you feel like a loser? Do you feel you need to learn more? Do you feel you need to take more action toward your aspirations? If you do, then act on it and study more, read and do whatever you need to educate your mind. For the present moment, accept whatever you know as part of you and know that you are just perfect right now at this very moment. You are lovable just as you are right now in this moment. You are just enough at this very moment. Whatever skillset that you want to gain for yourself to move your life and dreams forward, do that, and know you are growing. Feeling bad about yourself is counter-intuitive to your true growth.

Accept yourself just as you are right now at this very moment.

*

When someone dislikes you and you feel bad about it, it is another excellent opportunity for you to grow. For one reason or another, someone is likely dislike you at some point in your life. It happens to every human being, even saints!

If you have not caused them harm intentionally or unintentionally and someone just simply does not like you, the last thing you want to do is to try and get them to like you or feel bad that they do not like you.

Learning how to not let this get to you will help you on your journey to becoming the best version of you. If you try to get someone to like you, you will most likely end up doing something that is not authentically you. They either like you or don't and you should not try to fit into some mold for them to like you because you will move away from being your authentic self, which is the best version of you.

Another thing to see is that the person who doesn't like you has every right to feel whatever they feel. Someone disliking you has to do with who they are rather than who you are. It is something about you that they fear and fear it may exist in them. Their fear is not fact-based but their assumption. It may or may not be true.

Sometimes someone will dislike you because they judge a characteristic of yours to be unacceptable. My father hated the fact that I was a tomboy growing up. He thought girls should be feminine. I wasted so much energy feeling bad about my less than feminine nature. I love wearing pants and t-shirts. I feel very uncomfortable in a dress and girly shoes. I feel uncomfortable wearing jewelry. I judged myself to be less than a woman. Not too long ago, I made a simple decision. I am the way I am. I am just right, just the way I am as a woman. It is a waste of my energy to try and be softer. It is a waste of my energy to try and make a man feel smarter than me by staying quiet when I have a differing opinion. I like to argue and debate. All the ways that I am must be "being a woman" since I am a woman. This decision is new for me so I still have to remind myself from time to time when I feel bad about not acting the way my father had wanted me to act. The truth is trying to be something other than who I really am took up too much energy and, no matter how I tried, I could not change it. All that my attempts to change and my lack of self-acceptance took me away from who I was and took away my power to be all that I wanted to be: the best version of myself.

Let people have their opinions and judgments. Feel compassion for them. Then move away toward your free life and meet your joy.

There are times when someone will dislike you because they misunderstand you. This can be painful especially when the person who dislikes you is someone you care about deeply. You don't need to defend yourself. They will either see the truth or they won't. They have the right to make mistakes and make a wrong decision about you. You cannot afford your precious time and energy defending yourself for them to get a clearer understanding of you. They will or they won't. You have to tend to your own life. Tending to your own life is too important and you cannot waste your focus on defending yourself. It is not your job to set things right in their mind. No need. Your job is to find your path and stay on your path.

*

Learning to accept those who misunderstand you or wrongly accuse you or dislike you is not an easy thing to do. It is however very important for your self-growth so that you can be powerfully effective in doing your own work to make your world a better and more beautiful place.

Being misunderstood is so common for various reasons that you will have gained a great life skill by knowing how to just accept this condition as a part of life and move your focus to working on what you want to work on and being joyful living your authentic life.

We all want to be understood and accepted. We sometimes try to explain things and show people that they have misunderstood us or, at least, not fully understood us. There's also the related situation when they have made an unfair judgment about us, our reactions, or our actions.

You can spend a lot of time feeling frustrated at trying to get others to understand, to get a clearer idea, to see why you did what you did or made the choices that you made, but sometimes that just is not possible. Some people who you are trying to explain things to are simply not capable of understanding or at the least to try to understand you because they are not made that way and they just have no ability to do the understanding. They might even just lack empathy and do not even know that they should try and truly understand others. They just cannot.

I am sure we have all done this likely more than once but we get into an argument, the most unreasonable argument, feeling like we are going crazy because the person whom you are trying to communicate with and trying to clarify things with just seems to be making verbal noise.

You might even know from past experience with this person that they do not argue fairly, they kick you in the gut metaphorically, gaslight you, do whatever it takes to be right with no desire to seek truth or an honest understanding. They want to be right. They want the world to be portrayed in a way that is palatable for them. They want nothing that threatens their ego.

It is impossible to seek mutual truth with people like this. And you have to accept that they may even tell their version of the story with others just to bolster their ego, once again.

You know all of this yet, but you still engage with people like this sometimes just hoping that they will understand. But they won't. It is not because they are monsters or horrific human beings. They have injured souls and very afraid.

So what do you do in this kind of situation?

The only thing that you can do and must do if you want to be truly free of wasting time is to disengage from the argument and your need to have them understand as well as letting go of your concern about your reputation that this person may impact with their story that they feel they need to tell.

There is nothing that you can do to make them understand anything. There is nothing that you can do about what they may say about you. There is nothing that you can do about what they are thinking about you (if this is someone you care about in some way). You have no power to change anything, except…

You do have the power to influence what is going on inside you and in your own world. You do have the power to control that, you have the right to control it and you have the obligation to control it.

When you disengage, you have all that space and time available for your real stuff, your real life, your real passion, your real work, your real joy, and your real truth. Those things are what is truly important and you get to tend to them when you disengage from unreasonable conversations or arguments. Disengage!

*

If you are attracted to someone and they are not attracted to you, and you find yourself feeling bad about yourself, it is again another opportunity for you to discover very important tools that will make you grow and become happier.

It would be so nice if everyone who we liked and loved felt the same way toward us but this thing that we have the privilege to experience called life, is just not set up that way…unfortunately or not so unfortunately.

How we feel, how we move along this life is not about what is happening around us but what is happening inside of us and this is true every time.

So let's look at this situation you find yourself in. You are very attracted to someone. You would love it if they were attracted to you back, but they are not. You find yourself feeling unattractive in every way. You find yourself feeling unlovable, and not even worthy of love. You question if you are smart enough or even successful enough. You question everything about yourself because there must be something very wrong with you to explain why this person is not attracted to you.

Firstly, attraction does not work that way. Attraction is one of the most illogical things in this universe in that one can find oneself attracted to the utter opposite of one's values, desires, and life's goals. The person could be far from what you want, what you are normally attracted in terms of looks, far below your intelligence, accomplishments, confidence level, really all the conventional ways of judging someone can just be thrown out the window when it comes to attraction and even falling in love. Nothing really logically always makes sense when it comes to that department of human experience.

But there is a more important question that we must address here. That is about how you are feeling about yourself. The focus needs to be on how you are judging yourself and making decisions based on your worth and value and that is where you have a gem to gain here. You can discover, work through, process, learn, and gain new information about yourself so that you can then have a piece of really important self-knowledge.

It is important for your true happiness, sense of real fulfillment, and your sense of self that you learn this. That way you can also find that true love and healthy relationship with mutual attraction with someone who will be your perfect life partner. Without attaining this self-knowledge, it will be difficult for you to find the relationship that you really want and the healthy love that you really want.

So, for many good and even important reasons, you need to do some self-discovery into this bad feeling that you are having and learn some very important information.

So let's attack it:

- If you are judging yourself on your looks, thinking you are not good-looking enough or even unattractive because this person is not attracted to you that means that there is a part of you that is insecure about your looks. It is time now to accept your looks. This is not about making calculations and judgments about your looks. You may be conventionally attractive, according to the measuring sticks of the general public or media. But even if you are highly attractive according to those measuring sticks, you may still feel ugly or unattractive because of something inside you making you see yourself that way. The thing to realize is this: no matter where your looks fall in the spectrum, your sense of self-worth has to be based on your own reliable emotional source, which is complete and unconditional self-acceptance. It takes self-work to do this self-acceptance, but having that reliable source within yourself to just accept yourself unconditionally and love yourself unconditionally, and honor yourself unconditionally is really and truly worth everything. When you have that you have everything.

- And, in truth, that self-acceptance, or that level of unconditional self-acceptance can be applied to all the other areas that you're worrying about being deficient in.

- When you can simply and unconditionally accept yourself and your looks, what you are doing, and your success levels, your life has so much energy left over for you to play with. Think of all the energy you spend being self-critical that you could use.
- Doing all of this will automatically help you stop judging yourself as you have been doing with the person who does not reciprocate your attraction.
- But in addition to being able to be in a healthy relationship with yourself, in which you're unconditional accepted, it's about letting go and truly embracing your life. You will accept yourself unconditionally in every way, growing and learning and becoming more emotionally intelligent in the ways that need to that you can live your best life. You are having to do this very very important work on yourself, your life, your destiny, your world, your environment, all because of this painful feeling that you have been experiencing about this person.

When you stop judging yourself harshly, you will know to not take anyone's disinterest in you as a negative reflection on you. You realize that it is all a part of how the natural world exists. It is as simple as that.

*

When someone breaks up with you

When someone leaves you, it is very painful. It is one of the hardest things. There is no logic or analysis that can take the pain of it away quickly. It is however a time for you to discover some things about yourself. Of course, the first thing you have to do is properly grieve the loss and the pain of being left behind. Heartbreak feels sometimes like someone has died, and it is because the feeling of loss is that bad. So again, proper grieving is very important in the process of healing.

*

Once you have gone through much of the grieving process, and you will know when you are ready, take a look at how you are looking at this breakup. Try to see what kind of mindset you are practicing.

*

If you find yourself looking for ways to learn about yourself, about the relationship, and the breakup so that you can learn something useful about yourself and improve yourself so that you can prevent repeating the same mistakes in the next relationship and find happiness again, then you know that you have a growth mindset and you are going to heal in a healthy way. You are on the right track and you are doing fine.

*

However, you might find that you spend most of your time wondering why they could leave you and wondering how you can watch them suffer the pain that you are experiencing right now.

If you find yourself thinking of how you can get revenge for pain that they caused or just wishing to see them be in pain and you are unable to spend any time thinking of how you can learn something from the relationship, swinging from thinking it was all their fault to it was all your fault, if you cannot let go of the idea that it is over, if you can't let go of your ex, if you cannot stop to think of ways to become happy, if you feel that your life is now doomed, that you cannot find happiness again, and you find yourself settling into this very unhappy thinking… you know that you are experiencing a fixed mindset.

*

It is time for you to watch your mind, explore it, and work on opening your mind. Your mind is capable of learning to open and teach itself a growth mindset to help you learn and grow from this heartbreak, heal from your heartbreak and become a better, stronger, wiser and more loving (self-loving and loving others) person because you went through this heartbreak.

Heartbreak can be a powerful teacher for you if you let it. It is the most revealing time for parts of your personality, because you are so vulnerable. Since you are a bit broken, doing what you need to do to heal well, heal properly, heal powerfully, you can grow yourself in the process and reach for the best version of you.

"Most people are other people. Their thoughts are someone else's opinions, their lives a mimicry, their passions a quotation."

— Oscar Wilde

Chapter 7 - Why children need to be taught how to not take things personally

More than 75% of school shootings were committed by children who were bullied and could not figure out how to get help themselves.

*

What if they had been taught to think differently about the people around them? What if they were taught to love themselves by people outside of their home when it was not available for them at home?

What if we could teach children to think beyond just reacting? Teach them how to become more empathetic as well as to learn that they can tackle and conquer problems and challenges ?

What if we taught our children to be in a growth mindset instead of a fixed mindset?

What if we can help children get focused on proactive actions in life instead of just being a resentful victim of life?

I propose that we can prevent mass school shootings by focusing on teaching and healing our children.

What if we can? Isn't it worth discovering if we could prevent school shootings while helping to bring about happier, proactive, and positive adults in our world?

If you teach your children how to depersonalize judgments, you would be giving them a powerfully helpful tool against the negative influence of peer pressure.

If a child learns at a young age how to not let others' opinions matter to them, if they value their own opinions more, if they know their own self-worth and self-value, if they know that they are worthy of unconditional love, if they know how to love themselves, if they know how to look inwardly for values and not look outside for affirmation, they would not readily go and follow peer pressure.

*

Knowing how to not care what others think will give them tools for dealing with bullying.

If a child grows up with a strong sense of self-value, then he or she will know better what to do about bullying that they might be confronted with, whether it's about getting the right help or just knowing how to handle the situations in ways that are oriented toward problem-solving and peaceful resolution.

If a child feels a good and solid sense of self by having been taught to look inward, having been practicing looking inward, in combination with also being taught that they are enough, that they do not need the approval of their peers to feel ok, that they are worthy of love, that they love themselves, they will be more emotionally equipped to handle emotional challenges within themselves.

If they are being picked on, they would know what to do without taking it personally or thinking that something is wrong with them because they would have a strong sense of self.

With a strong sense of self, they would be empowered to live a more joyful life that is more emotionally independent and self-guiding.

*

If a child learns at a young age how to not let anyone get to him or her, what a freeing life, what a joy-filled life, what a truly self-loving life he or she would lead!

A child could learn at a young age how to be emotionally independent, to know that they are in charge of their own emotions.

Being emotionally independent they will be more emotionally skilled and, if they are more emotionally skilled, it would help them be more empathetic with themselves and others.

*

When a child learns at a young age how to turn inward to seek validation, to know how to know what is right and wrong, good and bad, valuable and not valuable, it is priceless.

If a child learns at a young age how to validate their own feelings and know how to be empathetic with themselves, they will also know how to feel empathetic with others. They will really know how to accept themselves in every moment. When a child has accepted themselves, they will be less likely to be impacted by bullying of any kind.

It will help them not only be more joyful humans but also better humans for a better world.

If a child learns how to not let people hurt their feelings, they will of course experience being joyful and better humans and they will make our world a better world because they will be better people.

*

It could prevent gun violence and other kinds of violence.

Some of the common factors in what makes a child become a shooter are the following:

1. They are abused at home.
2. They are neglected at home.
3. They are picked on by bullies in school.
4. They feel all alone.
5. They feel they do not belong.
6. They feel unlovable.
7. They feel unworthy of love.
8. They feel self-hatred.
9. They feel their bad feelings are caused by people around them.

If a child learns to become emotionally self-reliant, knowing how to rely on themselves for positive feedback or feedback about their own lives and what they are doing, they can be free to pursue the things that they believe in or do things that they want to do without the distractions of mood swings.

The health of our community and our world does take "a village", so if we as a community can help rescue these children who are in emotional danger and are left to their own devices, who may go on and hurt others (children and adults) in schools or in other "mass" settings, doesn't it make sense to reach out to help them?

*

Instead of allowing this to become a political issue and furthering ourselves from responsibility, we can do something about gun violence, by helping to heal our hurt children.

*

I will pledge right here on this page that if a school or a community wants me to come and help them organize this work, I am there.

Just contact me through my website:
www.healyourheartandfindyourlife.com.

I will be there to help you help your hurt children in your community.

"There is nothing enlightened about shrinking so that other people won't feel insecure around you. We are all meant to shine, as children do."

— Marianne Williamson

Chapter 8 - How doing this self-work is making a powerful difference in the healing of our world

---

Your work is to make this world a better place in your own way

As we take things personally we remain a part of the problems of our society, but as we begin taking responsibility for our own feelings and emotional state, we make our world a better place

- We won't blame others for our own negative feelings that prevent conflict with others.
- We will understand others without resentment, which also helps to improve relationships.

Doing this also helps to spread understanding and compassion.

- When you move your emotional self beyond the defensive position to truly understand yourself and the world that surrounds you, and when you began to get a greater understanding of humanity, you are going to be a person who carries within you deeper compassion and empathy for your fellow human beings and the condition of our world.

Doing this helps people get along well.

- Of course, when you have a deeper understanding of others around you without the defensive posturing, you are going to get along with people better.

- If everyone lived this way at all times, we definitely would be in a more peaceful and understanding world with better and deeper relationships.

Doing this helps to prevent problems that are caused by misunderstandings.

- Most of us walk around unaware how many misunderstandings take place in our lives. Misunderstandings are constantly taking place in and around our lives.
- We misunderstand visual cues.
- We misunderstand words due to the varying different experiences that each of us has had with those words yet we assume the meaning that we know, even if the person who is saying the word may have a very different experience with the word or words. What this ends up doing to us is causing misunderstandings, along with the emotional reactions that happen, then the judgments by both or more parties based on those judgements. Since many do not necessarily check in and ask what the meanings were in the first place, we all walk around thinking and believing the judgments that we made.

Doing this helps to help nurture and grow connections in our society.

- Of course, if each one of us moves beyond just judging or being judged, understanding one another in a more authentic truth-seeking manner. We are moving beyond the automatic hurt feelings and to actually understand, leading to the nurturing and growth of better connections in our society and in the wider world.

Doing this helps to solve violence and grows peaceful interactions.

- Of course, this would cause a reduction in violence since deeper understanding would take place before violence can happen. And since violence is due to misunderstanding or lack of understanding and lack of real connection, this would definitely lower violence and grow peaceful interactions in our society and in our world.

We are at a critical juncture. More than ever it appears that every one of us is needed to make this world a better place. We cannot afford complacency. We cannot wait for someone else to do the work. All of us have to participate. But doing this work is not hard. It is the most joyful thing being a part of making our world a better place.

The reason why it is the most joyful thing is that the first step in making this world a better place is making our inner world better, making our own self become the best version of ourselves.

When you work on becoming a person who is emotionally independent, you are making yourself the happiest person you can be and the most creative and successful person that you can be. When you walk through our world in that state, as the best version of you, you will automatically make this world a better place. Can you imagine a world full of people who are walking through life as the best version of themselves? It is a better world. It is the most beautiful world that we have yet to see.

"Few and mean as my gifts may be, I actually am, and do not need for my own assurance or the assurance of my fellows any secondary testimony."

— Ralph Waldo Emerson

Chapter 9 - Can you imagine a world?

Can you imagine a world with far less injustice, inequality, wars, terrorism, poverty, and all the other things that are ugly and bad today?

*

What if there was one thing that we could all do, one small thing that would alter our inner world and could chip away at all of those bad things and have a better world? What if there is? Would you alter that one small thing in your inner world to make it happen? What if this thing that we change in our inner world would not only will create a better world but also create a real and deep sense of happiness and joy in our own individual selves?

*

Would you make that one small change in your inner world?

*

What if changing that small thing in your inner world will take a bit of time because we have been in the practice of being the other way for so long, would you still begin learning to change that little thing in your inner world? Would it be worth your while to do it for yourself and, in turn, make a powerfully positive difference in your world?

*

As you practice this new habit, you will not only be making a powerful, positive change in yourself but also in our world. You are becoming a happier and kinder person and making this world a happier and kinder world.

I thank you from the bottom of my heart for making our world a more beautiful and better one, one person at a time, one day at a time, and one moment at a time.

About the Author

Nancy Sungyun grew up a California girl. At sixteen, she dove into a life of learning to master her emotional self. Her curiosity about learning technology led her to a master's degree in education at the University of Southern California. Her aspiration to guide others to healing led her to three years of life coach training from CoachU university, founded by Thomas Leanord.

Nancy coaches her clients to find their emotional skills mastery journey so that they can find their very best lives.

You can find out more about Nancy's work at www.healyourheartandfindyourlife.com.

Made in the USA
Monee, IL
29 July 2022